ATHENA

GREEK GODDESS OF WISDOM AND WAR

by Heather E. Schwartz

Content Consultant
Susan C. Shelmerdine, PhD,
Professor of Classical Studies
University of North Carolina, Greensboro
Greensboro, NC

CAPSTONE PRESS
a capstone imprint

Snap Books are published by Capstone Press,
1710 Roe Crest Drive, North Mankato, Minnesota 56003
www.mycapstone.com

Library of Congress Cataloging-in-Publication Data
Names: Schwartz, Heather E., author.
Title: Athena : Greek goddess of wisdom and war / by Heather E. Schwartz.
Description: North Mankato: Capstone Press, 2019. | Series: Snap Books.
   Legendary goddesses | Includes index.
Identifiers: LCCN 2018036723| ISBN 9781543554526 (library binding) |
ISBN 9781543559156 (pbk.) | ISBN 9781543554564 (ebook pdf)
Subjects: LCSH: Athena (Greek deity)—Juvenile literature.
Classification: LCC BL820.M6 S39 2019 | DDC 292.2/114—dc23
LC record available at https://lccn.loc.gov/2018036723

Editorial Credits
Gina Kammer, editor
Bobbie Nuytten, designer
Svetlana Zhurkin, media researcher
Katy LaVigne, production specialist

Image Credits
Alamy: PjrStudio, 27 (bottom), The History Collection, 14, The Picture Art
Collection, 4; Art Resource, NY: RMN-Grand Palais, 8; Bridgeman Images: The
Stapleton Collection/Private Collection/Erichthonius with Dragon's Feet or
Erittonio data in Guardia alle Figlie de Cecrope, Book II, illustration from Ovid's
Metamorphoses, Florence, 1832 (hand-colored engraving), Ademollo, Luigi, 10
(top); Dreamstime: Ksya, 7 (top); Getty Images: DEA/G. Dagli Orti, 9 (top), UIG/
Windmill Books/Brown Bear, 25; iStockphoto: duncan1890, 27 (top); Newscom:
Album/Fine Art Images, 5, 17, Album/Oronoz, 16 (bottom), Mavrixonline, 28,
UIG/Encyclopaedia Britannica, 16 (top); North Wind Picture Archives, 19, 29;
Shutterstock: Aerial-motion, 18 (top), Antracit, 21, breakermaximus, 6, Egor Bagrin,
cover, Elegant Solution, 15, f11photo, 20, Giedriius, 22 (bottom), irisphoto1, 23
(bottom), Josep Curto, 23 (top), Julia700702, 26, junrong, 9 (bottom), kostasgr, 18
(bottom), Marta Cobos, 22 (top), Masterrr, 12, 13, MatiasDelCarmine, 7 (bottom),
10 (bottom); The Metropolitan Museum of Art, Public Domain, 24

Design Elements by Shutterstock

TABLE OF CONTENTS

GODDESS OF WAR–AND MORE

Athena is best known as a goddess of war. During the Trojan War, she fought for the Greeks against the people of Troy. In one version of the myth, she helped the Greeks win their victory with her skills.

But though she had a strong sense of justice, she took on the Greeks for mainly personal reasons. She was angry after losing a contest judged by Paris, the Prince of Troy. Athena got competitive with her sister Aphrodite and aunt Hera. Each wanted to be named the most beautiful and bribed Paris in hopes of winning. Athena promised Paris victory in war. But Aphrodite won by offering to arrange a marriage between Paris and the most beautiful **mortal** woman on Earth. For Paris, this woman was Helen, wife to the king of Sparta. With Aphrodite's help, Paris stole Helen away. Angry with Aphrodite, Athena fought with the Greeks as they attacked Troy to bring Helen back. The goddess gave them courage. She swooped onto the battlefield, her armor flashing with lightning and the snakes on her shield breathing fire. Still, the city of Troy held strong.

Athena takes to the battlefield.

When a **seer** proclaimed that Troy would never be taken by force, Athena stepped in. Using her wise battle strategies, Athena gave the Greeks the idea to build a huge wooden horse. They gave the horse to Troy. Some of the Greek soldiers hid inside while the others sailed away. They pretended to be giving up so the Trojans would come out, thinking there was no more danger. Athena's plan was working until a Trojan priest figured out their trick. He wanted to have the horse destroyed, but Athena sent sea-serpents to kill him. Her plan continued. The Trojans brought the horse into their city. At night, all the Greeks returned. The soldiers inside the horse snuck out and let their army into Troy. The city fell to the Greeks, and Athena had her victory.

mortal—human, referring to a being who will eventually die

seer—someone who predicts things that will happen in the future

In ancient Greek myths, Athena is one of the Twelve Olympians, the most powerful gods and goddesses of ancient Greece. The myths are stories created for different kinds of purposes, such as teaching lessons or explaining events that happened in the natural world. In these stories, Athena generally favors brains over brawn. Athena is also the goddess of wisdom. In wars she taps into her wisdom to help her side win, as she did in the Trojan War.

While she has many positive traits and special powers, Athena is flawed in ways that make her seem almost human. She has been known to act out in jealousy and anger. In one myth, Athena was furious when Tiresias, son of a mortal and a **nymph**, saw her bathing. She struck him blind so he could never do it again. But Athena was also generous and forgiving. When Tiresias's mother begged the goddess to help him, Athena gave him the gift of **prophecy**. While Tiresias could no longer see the world around him, he could now see into the future.

nymph—a minor female goddess who lives on earth
prophecy—a foretelling of the future

6

Athena was also known in ancient Greece for her inventions. She invented tools including the rake, plow, and yoke to help farmers. She invented the flute, too, bringing a new style of music to the people of Greece. She didn't play the flute, herself, however. Legend has it she tried the instrument but gave it up. She didn't like the way her cheeks puffed out while playing it.

Smart, powerful, understanding, and helpful, Athena earned respect among both gods and mortals of ancient Greece.

Athena's Opposite

Ares, the Greek god of war, was more interested in the brutal aspects of battle than Athena was. This made him unpopular among the people. He was not even well liked by his own parents.

Athena was considered superior to Ares. More civil and just rather than bloodthirsty, she had a better approach to war.

HER FAMILY TREE

Only a mythical goddess can claim an origin story like Athena's. Some stories say she only had a father, Zeus. He was the king of all the Greek gods, or the **pantheon**. Other stories say Athena also had a mother, Metis. Metis was the goddess of good **counsel**.

Before Athena was born, Zeus's grandparents, Uranus and Gaia, told Zeus that Metis was going to give birth to a son who would grow up to dethrone him. Zeus did not want this to happen, of course. So one day he tricked Metis and swallowed her. After a time, Zeus developed a terrible headache. Athena was born from his head. She burst out of his forehead as a full-grown woman. She was even dressed in armor!

In one version of Athena's birth, the god Hephaistos strikes Zeus's head with his axe. Then Athena is born.

Did Zeus Really Marry His Own Sister?

The short answer is yes. But why? In Greek myths, it was common for Greek gods and goddesses to marry other family members. The gods were all relatives of Gaia, so marrying other gods often meant marrying siblings or other close family members. As part of myths, the gods did not have to follow the usual practices of humans.

counsel—support or advice
pantheon—all the gods of a particular mythology

Athena did not give birth to any children, but she raised Erichthonius, who was half-man and half-snake. He became a king.

Athena's father, Zeus, had many more children with both goddesses and mortals. In total, he had more than 30 children!

With so many siblings, Athena had a lot of competition for her father's attention. But by all accounts, Athena was her father's favorite. According to legend, he allowed her to use his weapons. That included his powerful thunderbolt, which he would throw like a spear to strike down his enemies.

Athena's family tree also included other famous **deities**. Her father's siblings included brothers Poseidon, god of the sea, and Hades, god of the underworld. Zeus also had sisters: Demeter, goddess of agriculture; Hestia, goddess of the hearth and home; and Hera, queen of the gods. These gods and goddesses were Athena's uncles and aunts. They were also among the Twelve Olympians.

deity—a god or goddess

forge—the special furnace in which metal is heated to be formed

THE 12 OLYMPIANS

ZEUS - king of the gods and god of the sky
APHRODITE - goddess of love and beauty
APOLLO - god of music
ARES - god of war
ARTEMIS - goddess of hunting
ATHENA - goddess of wisdom and war
DEMETER - goddess of agriculture
DIONYSUS - god of wine
HEPHAISTOS - god of fire and the **forge**
HERA - queen of the gods and goddess of marriage
HERMES - messenger and god of trade
POSEIDON - god of the sea

Hestia was sometimes considered one of the Twelve Olympians before Dionysus.

Athena's family tree

The goddess of wisdom and war never married and never had any children. However, Athena had plenty of aunts and uncles. She also had many half-siblings that were also children of Zeus to complete her powerful family of gods.

The god of the dead and the underworld was Athena's uncle, a brother of Zeus.

HADES

Athena's uncle Poseidon was the god of the sea.

POSEIDON

The king of the gods was Athena's father.

ZEUS

The goddess of agriculture was Athena's aunt.

DEMETER

The queen of the gods was Athena's aunt, but she was also the wife of Zeus.

HERA

Athena's aunt Hestia was the goddess of the home and hearth.

HESTIA

····· Parent
····· Zeus's siblings
····· Siblings

The messenger god was Athena's half-brother.

HERMES

Athena's half-sister was the goddess of love and beauty.

APHRODITE

Athena's half-brother was the god of prophecy, music, and healing.

APOLLO

The goddess of the hunt was Athena's half-sister.

ARTEMIS

The god of wine and festivals was Athena's half-brother.

DIONYSUS

ATHENA IN ACTION

Ancient Greek cities had patron deities to watch over them. One early king of Attika sought a patron for his city. The land was beloved of the gods, and Athena and Poseidon both wanted it. So there was a contest between Athena and Poseidon to see who would be the patron.

Athena faces Poseidon. Poseidon is often shown with his powerful trident, which he could use to break stone or cause earthquakes.

14

Poseidon went first and made a powerful move. He took up his **trident** and pushed it into the side of the Acropolis, a hill in the city. A stream of water flowed out. The people were delighted with his offering. Water was a valuable resource. Within moments, however, they realized it was sea water, salty and undrinkable.

Then it was Athena's turn. She created an olive tree. It could provide food and oil for the people. It could also provide wood for building as well as burning for heat and cooking. Her gift was clearly the superior one.

The people chose her as the winner. The city under her care was named Athens, in her honor.

What happened next depends on the story teller. In some versions, Poseidon happily agreed with the people of the city that Athena was the winner. In others, he was furious. He tried to fight Athena and flooded the city in anger.

trident—a long spear with three sharp points at its end

Like the story of Athens, many myths put Athena in conflict with other gods and goddesses and even humans. And she often acts with a combination of strength and wisdom. Athena helped Perseus kill Medusa, a monstrous creature with snakes for hair. She also helped Hercules throughout his life as he worked through a lengthy punishment. It involved performing 12 tasks, called Labors.

Athena helped Perseus kill Medusa by making sure he didn't look at Medusa directly. He would have been turned to stone if he had. But instead, he only saw her reflection in his shield.

But Athena didn't always act wisely or even kindly. In another myth, she felt threatened by human weaver Arachne's talent. The two competed to see who was more skilled. Athena wove four scenes. They showed the gods punishing mortals for believing they could be equal to gods. Arachne challenged her. She wove scenes that showed the gods abusing humans.

The scenes enraged Athena, and she could also see Arachne's work was much better than her own. Reacting in anger and jealousy, Athena turned Arachne into a spider. Arachne was condemned to weave for the rest of time—as a spider.

As these stories show, the Greek gods and goddesses weren't perfect. Athena and all the others had both virtues and shortcomings, just like humans.

Athena rages in jealousy against Arachne.

Parthenon

ancient theater

Acropolis

GODDESS FACT

The Parthenon was built on the Acropolis, a hill that rises 490 feet (150 meters) above Athens. The word *acropolis* means the high point of a city. Greeks often planned their cities around such hills on which they could build their most important buildings. The Athenian Acropolis is one of the most famous. It is made of limestone rock that dates back to the dinosaur age.

All About Athens

As far back as 3000 BC, Athens is the capital of Greece and one of the world's oldest cities. Known as the center of civilization, it's the site of the first democracy, where male citizens could vote to determine laws.

Today, Athens is best known as home to the Parthenon and for its Acropolis. The city also has 148 theatrical stages, the most in the world.

READY FOR BATTLE

Athena was always prepared to stand up for herself and fight for justice. Her appearance reflects her mission as a goddess in ancient Greece. Ready for battle, she wore a helmet and carried a spear and shield. Sometimes she carried an **aegis.** Her father, Zeus, lent it to her. In some stories, the aegis was a cloak. In others, it was a shield. It had the head of a monster called a **Gorgon** on it. When the aegis went into battle, the Gorgon roared terrifyingly.

The original statue of Athena inside the Parthenon is no longer standing. Copies of the statue have the goddess holding a spear. She is sheltering a snake with her shield. She wears a golden cloak. Her helmet is decorated with a **Sphinx** and two winged horses called Pegasi. Her breastplate is decorated with more snakes and the head of Medusa, a Gorgon.

A copy of the statue of Athena in the Parthenon stands in Nashville, Tennessee.

The symbols come from a myth. In the story, Athena assisted Perseus in slaying Medusa. Pegasus came from the blood of Medusa when Perseus beheaded the monster. Athena helped capture Pegasus so that another Greek hero could ride him. The winged horse is a symbol of strength and inspiration.

aegis—a shield or breastplate, or sometimes a leather cloak

Gorgon—a snake-haired woman whose appearance can turn people into stone

Sphinx—a winged creature with the body of a lion and the head of a woman

GODDESS FACT

According to Greek mythology, Pegasus later became a constellation and Zeus's servant.

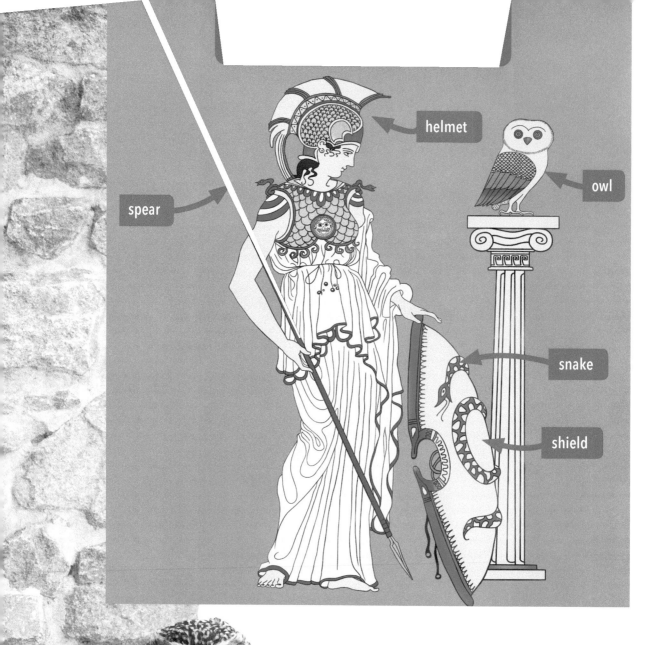

spear

helmet

owl

snake

shield

GODDESS FACT

The little owl associated with Athena is called *Athene noctua*. This is the modern scientific name for the owl species.

Other portrayals of Athena show her with an olive tree. The tree symbolizes how she won the city of Athens. Athena is also closely associated with the owl. The owl was a symbol of wisdom. Because of the owl's connection to Athena, Athens made it a symbol of the city. The bird appears on their coins.

A Symbol of War and Wisdom

The U.S. Military Academy adopted a coat of arms in 1898. The emblem was created to symbolize the Academy's motto, "Duty, Honor, Country."

Because Athena is associated with both war and wisdom, her helmet was included in the coat of arms. The symbol is carved on many of the Academy's buildings.

UNITED STATES

1802
2002

USA
34

MILITARY ACADEMY

2002

CELEBRATING ATHENA

In ancient Greece, the people of Athens looked forward to a huge summer celebration. It was called Panathenaea. Each year, they recited epic poems and played in musical contests. They competed in sports and watched horse races. They even sacrificed animals. The entire festival was for Athena. It was created to honor the city's patron goddess.

GODDESS FACT

In addition to celebrating Athena, the Panathenaea became Athens's answer to the Olympic Games. The Games were held in nearby Olympia.

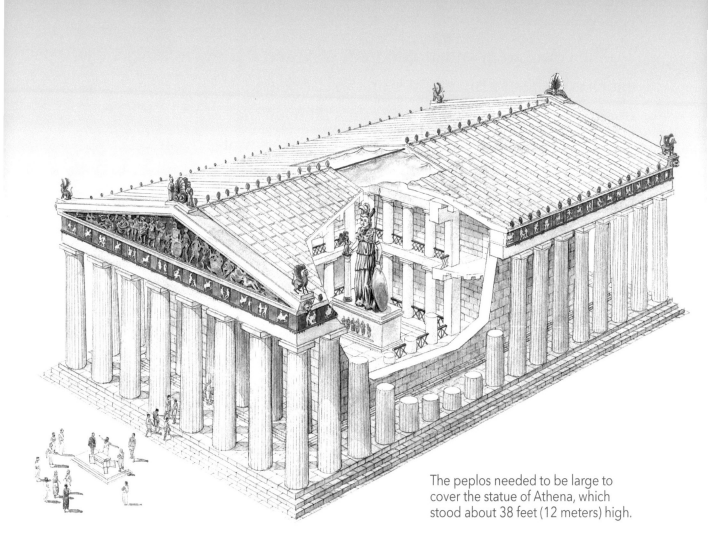

The peplos needed to be large to cover the statue of Athena, which stood about 38 feet (12 meters) high.

During the festival, the people walked together. They started at the city's largest gate. They stopped at the Parthenon. Inside, they gave a **peplos** to a tall wooden statue of Athena. The peplos was so enormous the people couldn't even carry it. It rode on the mast of a ship that was set on wheels.

peplos—an outer robe worn by women in ancient Greece

The celebration ended hundreds of years ago. But Athena's image lives on. She appears in ancient art displayed in museums all over the world. Statues, sculptures, and vase paintings illustrate the myths about her. They often show her wearing armor and holding an owl, a symbol of wisdom and the city of Athens.

Today, people celebrate the goddess Athena in other ways. They often show her as a strong character.

Athena also appears in ancient Greek literature, most famously the *Iliad* and the *Odyssey* by the Greek poet Homer. People still read these works today. In the *Iliad*, Athena is a war goddess. She is fiercely devoted to helping the Greeks win the Trojan War. In the *Odyssey*, Athena helps Odysseus and his son. She disguises herself as a friend they know. She also gets the other gods to help them. She talks about their troubles in meetings on Mount Olympus.

The *Iliad* is still famous today. Instead of listening to performances like in the days of ancient Greece, now most people read it to learn the story.

GODDESS FACT

Athena was featured on an ancient coin that was distributed in the city of Corinth. The other side of the coin pictured the winged horse, Pegasus.

Today, people don't celebrate Athena the way they did during ancient times. But she has not been forgotten. Her stories are still being retold. In 1981 the movie *Clash of the Titans* told the tale of the Greek hero Perseus. There was a remake of the movie in 2010. Both movies featured Athena. She sent an owl to help Perseus on his quest. In 1997 Athena was in the Disney movie *Hercules*. She was also on the TV show *Hercules: The Animated Series* and appears in Rick Riordan's Percy Jackson book series.

Rick Riordan's *The Mark of Athena* was published in 2012. In the story, the main characters have to find an ancient, stolen statue of Athena.

The stories about Athena may be ancient Greek myths, but they continue to inspire people. Even now, she stands for bravery, wisdom, justice, and strength in the modern world.

Literature as Life

When they were performed, the stories of the *Iliad* and the *Odyssey* were considered more than entertainment. Ancient Greeks listened to them as part of religious festivals. They admired characters in the stories for their heroism. The stories were told through song over and over again.

Today, people read the *Iliad* and the *Odyssey* as classic works of literature. They are windows into life in ancient Greece.

GLOSSARY

aegis (AY-juhs)—a shield or breastplate, or sometimes a leather cloak

counsel (KOUN-suhl)—support or advice

deity (DEE-uh-tee)—a god or goddess

forge (FORJ)–the special furnace in which metal is heated to be formed

Gorgon (GOR-guhn)—a snake-haired woman whose appearance can turn people into stone

mortal (MOR-tuhl)—human, referring to a being who will eventually die

nymph (NIMF)—a minor female goddess who lives on earth

pantheon (PAN-thee-on)— all the gods of a particular mythology

peplos (PEH-pluhs)—an outer robe worn by women in ancient Greece

prophecy (PROF-uh-see)—a foretelling of the future

seer (SEE-uhr)—someone who predicts things that will happen in the future

Sphinx (SFINGKS)—a winged creature with the body of a lion and the head of a woman

trident (TRY-dent)—a long spear with three sharp points at its end

READ MORE

Loh-Hagan, Virginia. *Athena*. Gods and Goddesses of the Ancient World. Ann Arbor, Mich.: Cherry Lake Publishing, 2017.

O'Connor, George. *Olympian's Boxed Set*. New York: First Second, 2014.

Riordan, Rick. *Percy Jackson's Greek Gods*. Los Angeles: Disney-Hyperion, 2014.

Temple, Teri. *Athena: Goddess of Wisdom, War, and Crafts*. Greek Gods and Goddesses. Mankato, Minn.: Childs World, 2019.

INTERNET SITES

Use FactHound to find Internet sites related to this book.

Visit *www.facthound.com*

Just type in 9781543554526 and go!

 Check out projects, games and lots more at **www.capstonekids.com**

INDEX